Who is GOD? Who am I? Why am I Here?

PREPARED BY:

MARIAN DAVENPORT

By Marian Davenport

ISBN# 978-0-9962410-3-8

Bible References

All scriptures are from
New King James Version
New Spirit-Filled Life Bible
copyright© 2002 by Thomas Nelson, Inc., unless noted

The Living Bible TLB
copyright© 1971

New Living Translation NLT
copyright© 1996, 2004, 2007
by Tyndale House Foundation

Categories: Christian, Mentor or Making Disciples material

Publisher: Royal Scribes Publishing

Facebook: Marian Davenport, Author
Email: writethevisions@gmail.com

Graphic Design by Holly Hyde of Posy Creative

DEDICATION

This book is dedicated to our Connect Group who
encouraged the work, and agreed it is needed.
To Dolly Elswick who helped gather the scriptures,
and to Holly Hyde for all of her help.

THOUGHTS FOR A MENTOR

Who is God? Who am I? Why am I here?

This little book is a quick resource to cover the foundational truths of the Bible. Through scriptures it answers the 'who and why' questions many are asking, but they don't know how to find them in the Bible.

Ideally, one or two people, who would like to know the answers to these questions, will join a person who will mentor, or guide them through the scriptures.

Have a Bible handy so you can look up some of the verses together. That will help them learn how to use the Word for themselves. Encourage the person to memorize some of the verses.

The Word will naturally spark questions. Take time to relate the scriptures to their life and show them how just knowing the truth inspires answers.

Have fun. Pray together. Be alert to recognize when Jesus answers. Make a new friend. It's exciting to help someone discover who God is, who we are, and why we're here!

table of
CONTENTS

"When you know the truth, the truth will set you free." – John 8:32

CHAPTER ONE
Knowing God, Knowing Me

Who is God? Who am I?

What a profound question. Is there an answer? Yes.

When God, the Creator of the universe spoke, his words became the foundation of human history. In his Word, the Bible, we can find the right answer to all of our questions.

> *When you know the truth, the truth will set you free.*
> (John 8:32)

So, we will search God's Word to find the truth of who he is, and who we are. And in the process we'll learn why we're here. Then, by faith, we trust what the Scriptures say, and choose to live by the rich promises they hold.

"I have hidden the Word in my heart that I might not sin against God." – Psalm 119:11

CHAPTER TWO
The Bible

One of the most precious treasures God gave us is his Word, the Bible. It is the human's manual that can direct our path, and teaches us how to live the life he created for us. We could call it, "God's How-To Book." But it doesn't do us any good if we don't know what it says.

Psalm 119:11 NLT says, *I have hidden the Word in my heart that I might not sin against God.*

God's Word is the truth. When we're confused, the Word can give us the wisdom and understanding needed for the best solution. If we seek God's will, he will reveal the path to success in every area of life.

Here are a few verses to give insight into the value of God's Word.

> *Your Word is very pure. Therefore, your servants love it.*
> (Psalm 119:140)
>
> *Great peace have those who love your Word. And nothing causes them to stumble.* (Psalm 119:165)

. . . You give me understanding according to your Word.
(Psalm 119:169)

. . . The Word of the Lord endures forever. (I Peter 1:25)

Heaven and earth will disappear, but my words will never disappear. (Matthew 25:35 NLT)

Jesus said, *". . . People do not live by bread alone, but by every word that comes from the mouth of God."* (Matthew 4:4 NLT)

All scripture is inspired by God and is useful to teach us what is true and to make us realize what is wrong in our lives. It corrects us when we are wrong and teaches us to do what is right. (2 Timothy 3:16 NLT)

What is Faith?

The Bible tells us in Hebrews 11:1, *Now faith is the substance of things hoped for, the evidence of things not seen.*

Faith comes by hearing and hearing by the Word of God.
(Romans 10:17)

By faith, we choose to believe God's Word is true. Sounds simple. But there's a problem. Let's look at that before we go any further.

CHAPTER THREE
The Problem

By human nature, we want to be the person in charge of our life. We don't understand that God's principles were created to bless us and help us find his love. Such attitudes aren't unique, but the Bible calls them sin.

Isaiah 52:6 NLT tells us, *All of us, like sheep, have strayed away, we have left God's paths to follow our own way.*

I John 1:8 adds, *If we say we have no sin, we deceive ourselves, and the truth is not in us.*

Sin hinders our privilege of having a close relationship with God. It causes us to fear God instead of love him. Our pride challenges us to live our life outside of his will.

All have sinned and fall short of glory of God. (Romans 3:23)

Isaiah 59:2 NLT says, *It's your sins that have cut you off from God. Because of your sins, he has turned away and will not listen anymore.*

When our relationship to God isn't right it causes PROBLEMS in all areas of life. Everyone has problems, but too often, we come up with our own plan on how to cope.

There is a way that seems right to a man, but its end is the way of death. (Proverbs 16:25)

Giving up bad habits, being a good person, going to church, and sharing our money is good, but they don't make us right with God. There's only one way to be right with God.

Jesus Christ said, *"I am the way, the truth, and the life. No one comes to the Father, except through me.* (John 14:6)

CHAPTER FOUR

The Solution

God sent his one and only son, Jesus, to earth as a human to make the way for us to have fellowship with our heavenly Father, God. Jesus surrendered his life for us and took care of our sin problem.

> *For the wages of sin is death, but the gift of God is eternal life in Christ Jesus our Lord.* (Romans 6:23)

> *But God demonstrated his own love toward us, in that while we were still sinners, Christ died for us. Romans 5:8*

You see, God was on one side and all people were on the other side. Jesus came as a go-between to bring them together, by giving his life for all mankind.
(I Timothy 2:5 interpretation)

Yes, Jesus sacrificed his divine life to restore our relationship with him. Now we, as individuals, must choose to accept what he did for us. Such knowledge always requires a response. What will we do with what we know now?

> *By grace you are saved through faith; and that not of yourselves; it is the gift of God.* (Ephesians 2:8)

OUR RESPONSE

We choose to believe by faith that Jesus paid the price for our sins through his death, and that he rose from the dead and is alive today. We admit God has not been first place in our life and ask him to forgive us of our sins.

> *If we confess our sins, he is faithful and just to forgive us our sins and to cleanse us from all unrighteousness.* (I John 1:9)

> Romans 10:9 says, *If you confess Jesus is your Lord, and you believe in your heart that God has raised him from the dead, you will be saved.*

> *There is salvation in no one else! God has given no other name under heaven by which we must be saved.* (Acts 4:12 NLT)

> *For by grace you have been saved through faith, and that not of yourselves; it is the gift of God, not of works, lest anyone should boast.* (Ephesians 2:8-9)

> *But to all who believed him and accepted him, he gave the right to become children of God. They are reborn, not with a physical birth resulting from human passion or plan, but a birth that comes from God.* (John 1:12-13 NLT)

Yes, step one is to accept the truth of God's Word, repent of our sins, and invite the Holy Spirit to have control of our lives. The Word says, *I stand at the door and knock. If anyone hears my voice and opens the door, I will come in to him and dine with him, and he with me.* (Revelation 3:20)

> *Whoever calls upon the name of the Lord will be saved.* (Romans 10:13)

WE ACCEPT GOD'S FREE GIFT OF SALVATION.

SALVATION PRAYER

Father God, on this date_____,I confess I have sinned

against you by doing my own thing, and I ask you to forgive me of all my sin.

I choose to invite you to come into my life and help me become the person

you created me to be. Thank you for making the way for me to be free from

the past, so I can step into the future you have for me. Amen.

"Old things have passed away and behold all things become new." – 2 Cor. 5:17-20

CHAPTER FIVE
Who is God?

Wonderful! Jesus is now your Savior. A new life has begun. *Old things have passed away and behold all things are become new.* (2 Corinthians 5:17-20) When we become a Christian we become a brand new person inside. A new life begins.

So, step one is to accept the truth of God's Word, repent of our sins, and invite the Holy Spirit to have control of our life. But who is this God to whom we've given control? Let's get acquainted with what his book tells us about him.

God almighty, the Creator of the universe is enthroned in the heavens, yet he's right here with us, and he is concerned about every detail of our lives. He is called by many names. Here are a few of them.

> *God is love.* (I John 4:8)

No other ruler in history has been described as love, but our God's name is LOVE. Everything about his character comes from his heart of love.

We understand so little about real love in our world. Not that there aren't loving people, lovely places, and much to love. But the word says God IS love. The environment of his Kingdom is saturated with his pure, unadulterated love. His loving presence has the power to heal hurt emotions, and fill us so full of his presence we want nothing more than him.

To find God is to find Love, which makes it possible for our hearts to change so we are able to love others through his love in us.

God is Holy - The Word says, *Be holy because I am holy.* (I Peter 1:16) What an amazing thought - but how can a human become holy like God?

We've learned Jesus paid the price for our sins. As we gain knowledge of the Word, we begin to recognize the things in our lives that don't honor God. Then we quickly surrender each hindrance to him. Mentally, yet from the heart, we give everything in our life that doesn't match the truth of who the Bible says we are, to God. We take all the good, bad, and ugly in our life, and lay it at his feet.

God is pleased when we do this. Here is a verse that reveals how he sees us after we accept Jesus as our Savior.

> *You are a chosen people. You are royal priests, a holy*
> *nation. God's very own possession.* (I Peter 2:9a)

God is Omnipresent –meaning always everywhere. We can never get away from his presence. Psalm 139:8-14 NLT reads, *If I go to heaven you are there; if I go down to the grave you are there. If I ride the wings of the morning, if I dwell by the farthest oceans, even there your hand will guide me, and your strength will support me, I could ask the darkness to hide me and the light* *around me to become night but even in darkness I cannot hide from you. To you the night shines as bright as day. Darkness and light are the same to you.*

The unfailing love of the Lord fills the earth.
(Psalm 33:5 NLT)

The one who descended is the one who ascended higher than all the heavens, so that he might fill the entire universe with himself. (Ephesians 4:10 NLT)

"I am a God near at hand," says the Lord, and not a God afar off. Can anyone hide himself in secret places. So I shall not see him?" Do I not fill heaven and earth?" (Jeremiah 23:23-24)

One angel cried to another, "Holy, holy, holy is the Lord of hosts; the whole earth is full of his glory!" (Isaiah 6:3)

He who descended is also the One who ascended far above all the heavens, that he might fill all things.
(Ephesians 4:10)

He loves righteousness and justice; the earth is full of the goodness of the Lord. (Psalm 33:5)

God is Omnipotent – meaning unlimited authority or power.
Although God is so mighty he spoke the universe into existence (Genesis 1), he wants to be very personal to each of us. He delights in helping us be successful in everything we put our hands to. (Deuteronomy 28:8)

Behold, I am the Lord, the God of all flesh. Is there anything too hard for Me? (Jeremiah 32:28)

Jesus said, *"With men this is impossible, but with God all things are possible."* (Matthew 19:26)

For with God nothing will be impossible. (Luke 1:37)

I pray. . . that you will know what is the exceeding greatness of his power toward us who believe, according to the working of his mighty power. (Ephesians 1:16, 19)

God is Omniscient - He has all knowledge, understanding, and perceives all things.

The Bible is full of verses about God's all-knowing ways. Job said, *The One who is perfect in knowledge is with you.* (Job 36:4)

Luke 12:7 tells us he knows the number of hairs on our head. Hebrews 4:13 says all things are naked and open before him. Matthew 6:31-32 commands us not to worry about anything because our heavenly Father knows our needs.

Psalm 139:1-4 is another great verse. *O Lord, you have searched me and known me. You know my sitting down and my rising up, you understand my thoughts afar off. You comprehend my path and my lying down, and are acquainted with all my ways. For there is not a word on my tongue, but behold, O Lord, you know it.*

It's encouraging to read about who God is. Here are some other scriptures to look up on him being omniscient. Psalm 44:21, Psalm 147:4-5, Romans 11:33-34, Psalm 33:13-15.

God is called Father

We know there is only one God, the Father, who created everything, and we live for him. . . (I Corinthians 8:6 NLT)

No matter what our earthly father is or was like, God, as our Father, loves us with his everlasting love.

> *. . . He will never leave us or forsake us.*
> *(Deuteronomy 31:6 NLT)*

> *He is like a father to us, tender and sympathetic to those who reverence him. (Psalm 103:13 TLB)*

God the Trinity

Another intriguing characteristic of God is the fact that he is three persons in one. We call them the Trinity; three entities made up of God the Father, his son, Jesus, and his Holy Spirit.

> *May the grace of the Lord Jesus Christ, and the love of God, and the fellowship of the Holy Spirit be with you all. (2 Corinthians 13:14)*

"God so loved the world that he gave his only son that whoever believes in him should not perish but have everlasting life." – John 3:16

CHAPTER SIX
Jesus, God's Son

○ ○ ○ ○ ○ ○ ○ ○

God wanted fellowship with his children, but people turned from his plan, and chose to go their own way. This was no surprise to our all-knowing God.

His holiness required a pure sacrifice to reunite those he loved to himself. He wanted fellowship with his people like he had with Adam and Eve in the garden before they sinned. (Genesis 2:4-3:20)

So God sent his son, Jesus, as a baby, born to a woman on earth to be the Savior of the world. Jesus was the only perfect one who had no sin.

Jesus was fully God and fully man. He lived a pure life. Around age thirty, he began to declare that the kingdom of God had come. He taught the truth of the Bible, and revealed himself to be God's son. He proved that truth by performing many miracles such as healing people (Matthew 8:2-3, Mark 8:22-26, Mark 9:14-23), raising the dead (Luke 7:11-17, John 11:38-44), and casting out demons. (Mark 5:1-20, Matthew 8:28-34).

Three years later, he took our place on a cross, shed his blood, and was crucified. He died as the perfect sacrifice for man's sins. Yours and mine. Good Friday represents the day he was crucified.

However, three days later he came out of the grave alive, proving death could not hold him. We celebrate the glory of his resurrection on Easter Sunday.

> *God so loved the world that he gave his only Son that whoever believes in him should not perish but have everlasting life.* (John 3:16)

> *We see Jesus, who was given a position a little lower than the angels; and because he suffered death for us, he is now crowned with glory and honor. Yes, by God's grace, Jesus tasted death for everyone.* (Hebrews 2:9 NLT)

Here are some of the highlights of Psalm 103. The Lord forgives all our sins, heals all our diseases, redeems our life from destruction, and crowns us with loving kindness and tender mercies. Our mouth is satisfied with good things, and our youth is renewed like the eagles. He executes righteousness and justice for all who are oppressed. The Lord is merciful and gracious, slow to anger and abounding in mercy.

> *Jesus is our wonderful Counselor, Mighty God, Eternal Father, Prince of Peace.* (Isaiah 9:6)

Jesus is the Word

> *In the beginning was the Word and the Word was with God and the Word was God. . . . All things were made through him and without him nothing was made that was made.* (John 1:1-3)

Jesus is Savior

For God took the sinless Christ and poured into him our sins. Then, in exchange, he poured God's goodness into us. (2 Corinthians 5:21 TLB)

Jesus is the Life and Light

In him was life, and the life was the light of men. And the light shined in the darkness and the darkness did not comprehend it. (John 1:4-5)

Jesus is Love

Who shall separate us from the love of Jesus? Shall tribulation, or distress, or persecution, or famine, or nakedness, or peril, or sword? Yet in all these things we are more than conquerors through him who loves us. For I am persuaded that neither death nor life, nor angels, nor principalities, nor powers, nor things present, nor things to come, nor height, nor depth, nor any other created thing, shall be able to separate us from the love of God which is in Christ Jesus our Lord. (Romans 8:35, 37-39)

Jesus is a Husband

For your Maker is your husband, the Lord of hosts is his name. (Isaiah 54:5)

For I am jealous for you with godly jealousy. For I have betrothed you to one husband, that I may present you as a chaste virgin to Jesus Christ. (2 Corinthians 11:2)

They broke their covenant to Me though I was a husband to them, says the Lord. (Jeremiah 31-32)

Jesus is a Friend

Jesus said, Now, I call you not servants; for a servant doesn't know what his lord does; but I have called you friend; for all things that I have heard of my Father I have made known to you. (John 15:15)

Jesus has All Authority

Jesus said, "All authority has been given to me in heaven and on earth." (Matthew 28:18)

God put all things under Jesus feet, and gave him to be head over all things to the church. (Ephesians 1:22)

Jesus said He is "I Am"

I am the resurrection and the life. He who believes in Me, though he may die, he shall live. And whoever lives and believes in me shall never die. (John 11:25)

I am the way, the truth, and the life, no one comes to the Father except through Me. (John 14:6)

I am the bread of life. He who comes to Me shall never hunger, and he who believes in me shall never thirst. (John 6:35)

I am the Good Shepherd. The Good Shepherd gives his life for the sheep. (John 10:11)

I am with you always, even to the end of the age.
(Matthew 28:20b)

I am the Alpha and the Omega, the beginning and the End; the First and the Last. (Revelation 22:13)

"I am with you always, even to the end of the age." - Matthew 28:20b

"You will receive power when the Holy Spirit comes upon you. And you will be my witnesses, telling people about me everywhere..." – Acts 1:8 NLT

CHAPTER SEVEN

God, the Holy Spirit

J esus said, *I will ask the Father and he will give you another Comforter, and he will never leave you. He is the Holy Spirit, the Spirit who leads into all truth. The world at large cannot receive him, for it is looking for him and doesn't recognize him. But you do, for he lives with you now. . .*
(John 14:16–18 TLB)

"I tell you the truth, it is to your advantage that I go away; for if I do not go away, the Helper will not come to you, but if I go, I will send him to you. (John 16:7)

God raised Jesus from the dead, and we are all witnesses of this. Now he is exalted to the place of highest honor in heaven, at God's right hand. And the Father, as he had promised, gave him the Holy Spirit to pour out upon us. . . (Acts 2:32-33 NLT)

The Holy Spirit is our Guide

Jesus said, . . . When the Holy Spirit of truth comes, he will guide you into all truth. He will not speak on his own, but will tell you what he has heard. He will tell you about the future. He will bring me glory by telling you whatever he receives from me. (John 16:13-14 NLT)

The Holy Spirit Makes His Home in Us

You were included in Christ when you heard the message of truth, the gospel of your salvation. When you believed, you were marked in him with a seal, the promised Holy Spirit, who is a deposit guaranteeing our inheritance until the redemption of those who are God's possession, to the praise of his glory. (Ephesians 1:13-14)

. . . by our faith, the Holy Spirit helps us with our daily problems and in our praying. For we don't even know what we should pray for, nor how to pray as we should; but the Holy Spirit prays for us with such feeling that it cannot be expressed in words. And the Father who knows all hearts knows, of course, what the Spirit is saying as he pleads for us in harmony with God's own will. And we know that all that happens to us is working for our good if we love God and are fitting into his plans. (Romans 8:26 - 28 NLT)

Don't you realize that your body is the temple of the Holy Spirit, who lives in you and was given to you by God? You do not belong to yourself, for God bought you with a high price. So you must honor God with your body. (I Corinthians 6:19 NLT)

The Holy Spirit Brings Gifts

For his Spirit searches out everything and shows us God's deep secrets. No one can know a person's thoughts except that person's own spirit, and no one can know God's thoughts except God's own Spirit. And we have received God's Spirit (not the world's spirit), so we can know the wonderful things God has freely given us. (I Corinthians 2:12)

I Corinthians 12:4-11 NLT describes the varieties of gifts given by God's Spirit. First, we're reminded that no one can say Jesus is Lord, except by the Holy Spirit. Then it goes on to explain that spiritual gifts are given to each of us.

To one person, the Spirit gives the ability to give wise advice. Someone else may be especially good at studying and teaching, and this is his gift from the same Spirit. He gives special faith to another, and to someone else the power to heal the sick. He gives power for doing miracles to some, and to others power to prophesy and preach. . . (I Corinthians 12:8-9 TLB)

The Holy Spirit Gives Power

You will receive power when the Holy Spirit comes upon you. And you will be my witnesses, telling people about me everywhere. . . (Acts 1:8 NLT)

The Holy Spirit Gives Fruit

The fruit of the Spirit is love, joy peace, patience, kindness, goodness, faithfulness, gentleness, and self-control. Against such things there is no law. (Galatians 5:22-23)

The Holy Spirit Gives Boldness

A story in Acts 4:31 tells us, *"And when they prayed, the place where they were assembled together was shaken, and they were all filled with the Holy Spirit, and they spoke the word of God with boldness."*

After Jesus ascended to heaven, the Holy Spirit introduced himself to the people. In Acts 2:2-5 we read of a roaring wind filling the house. Then what looked like flames or tongues of fire appeared and settled on them. Everyone was filled with the Holy Spirit and began speaking in other languages as the Holy Spirit gave them the ability.

This phenomenon is often called "speaking in tongues", or "being filled with the Spirit with the evidence of tongues." The gift of the Spirit is available to all people who have received Jesus as Savior. Speaking in an unknown language confirms the Holy Spirit is actively moving in our lives. It enhances our prayer life. As we yield to the Spirit praying through us, we're interacting with the unseen Kingdom of God.

In this scripture from Acts, some of the people spoke languages they had never learned, but others understood what they were saying. This could have been a foreign language, or a currently unknown language. Some believers think we may sometimes be speaking the language of angels. Whichever it is, speaking in other tongues is a supernatural ability the Holy Spirit brings as we yield to his will to be filled with the Holy Spirit.

"You are the light of the world. A city that is set on a hill cannot be hidden."
– Matthew 5:14

CHAPTER EIGHT
Who am I?

∘ ∘ ∘ ∘ ∘ ∘ ∘ ∘

So the question becomes, "Who am I after I accept Jesus as my Savior?"

Think about it. Jesus' presence is living in us, and the Kingdom of God is all around. When we become believers of Jesus, meaning we place our faith in him for salvation, we are born anew by the Spirit of God. We become a new creation in Jesus Christ, old things pass away, all things become new. (2 Corinthians 5:17)

We also receive eternal life, meaning when our physical bodies give out, we'll have a new life with Jesus in heaven.

Jesus ascended to heaven and is seated at the right hand of God, and he saved a place for us to sit with him on his throne.

WHO AM I?

The Word tells us who we are when we receive Jesus as Savior.

I am God's Child

> *Having been born again, not of corruptible seed but incorruptible, through the Word of God which lives, and abides forever.* (I Peter 1:23)

I am Forgiven

> *He is so rich in kindness and grace that he purchased our freedom with the blood of his Son and forgave our sins. He has showered his kindness on us, along with all wisdom and understanding.* (Ephesians 1:7-8 NLT)

I am a New Person

> *Therefore, if anyone is in Christ, he is a new creation; old things have passed away; behold, all things have become new.* (2 Corinthians 5:17)

I am Delivered from the Power of Darkness

> *He has rescued us from the kingdom of darkness and transferred us into the kingdom of his dear Son, who purchased our freedom and forgave our sins.* (Colossians 1:13-14 NLT)

I am Blessed

You might enjoy reading Deuteronomy 28:1-14. It's an amazing example of the blessings that belong to a child of God. Of course, we can miss these promises if we don't know they belong to us. To reap their benefits we choose to say, "Yes, Lord. Those words are my promises from you." Then, by faith, we thank him for all the good gifts he has stored up for us, and watch for them to come. (Philippians 4:6)

> *For I know the thoughts I think toward you, says the Lord, thoughts of peace and not of evil, to give you a future and a hope.* (Jeremiah 29:11)

> *Blessed be the God and Father of our Lord Jesus Christ, who has blessed us with every spiritual blessing in the heavenly places in Christ Jesus.* (Ephesians 1:3)

> *All things work for good to those who love God and are called according to his purposes.* (Romans 8:28)

I am Holy

My first thought is, "Really? Accepting Jesus makes me holy? I don't feel very holy." Of course we don't. We know who we really are. But God's Word says Jesus' sacrifice paid the price for us to be pure, holy vessels, fit for God's good purposes. Our part is to believe this truth.

We bring the areas in our life we know don't please the Holy Spirit, those hindrances that keep us from living in the fullness of who the Word says we are, and ask him to take them from us.

He is able to replace our hate with his love, and remove anger and give us patient kindness. Or he will take our pride, which is powered by fear, and give us a humble spirit who thinks of others as better than themselves.

> *Think clearly and exercise self-control. . . Don't slip back into your old ways of living to satisfy your own desires. You didn't know any better then. But now you*

must be holy in everything you do, just as God who chose you is holy. For the Scriptures say, "You must be holy because I am holy." (I Peter 1:13-16 NLT)

To live the holy life he has provided, we repent for our negative characteristics and ask God to replace them with his virtues.

I am God's Workmanship

We are God's masterpiece. He has created us anew in Christ Jesus, so we can do the good things he planned for us long ago. (Ephesians 2:10)

I am the Light of the World

You are the light of the world. A city that is set on a hill cannot be hidden. (Matthew 5:14)

I am Free

*Jesus said . . . "If you abide in my word, you are my disciples. And you shall know the truth, and the truth shall make you free."
. . . Therefore if the Son makes you free, you shall be free indeed. (John 8:31, 36)*

I am a Conqueror

. . . Yet in all these things we are more than conquerors through him who loved us. (Romans 8:37)

I am Sealed with the Holy Spirit

. . . having believed, you were sealed with the Holy Spirit of promise. (Ephesians 1:13)

I am Complete

> *You are complete in him, who is the head of all principality and power.* (Colossians 2:10)

I am a Child of God

> *What great love the Father has lavished on us, that we should be called children of God. And that is what we are.* (I John 3:1)

I am Free from Condemnation

> *So now there is no condemnation for those who belong to him, the power of the life-giving Spirit has freed you from the power of sin that leads to death.* (Romans 8:1-2a NLT)

> *He has removed our sins as far away from us as the east is from the west.* (Psalm 103:12 TLB)

Our sins are forgiven just as if they never happened. We must remember this truth when our mind is tried by other voices wanting to pull us into thinking about who we were before.

I am Being Changed into His Image

> *Being confident of this very thing, that he who has begun a good work in you will complete it until the day of Jesus Christ.* (Philippians 1:6)

> *But we all, with unveiled face, beholding as in a mirror the glory of the Lord, are being transformed into the same image from glory to glory by the Spirit of the Lord.* (2 Corinthians 3:18)

THE WORD SAYS I HAVE

I Have Access to Father God

Jesus, our High Priest understands our weaknesses, for he faced all of the same testings we do, yet he did not sin. So let us come boldly to the throne of our gracious God. There we will receive his mercy, and we will find grace to help us when we need it most. (Hebrews 4:15-16 NLT)

I Have Overcome

Whatever is born of God overcomes the world. This is the victory that overcomes the world—our faith. (1 John 5:4)

I Have Everlasting Life

Jesus said, "I tell you the truth, those who listen to my message and believe in God who sent me have eternal life. They will never be condemned for their sins, but they have already passed from death into life. (John 5:24 NLT)

For the law of the Spirit of life in Christ Jesus has made me free from the law of sin and death. (Romans 8:2)

I Have God's Peace

The peace of God, which surpasses all understanding, will guard your hearts and minds through Christ Jesus. (Philippians 4:7)

I Have Everything I Need

My God shall supply all my needs according to his riches in glory by Christ Jesus. (Philippians 4:19)

THE WORD SAYS I CAN

I Can Do All Things

*I can do all things through Christ who strengthens me.
(Philippians 4:13)*

I Can Forget the Past

I do not count myself to have apprehended; but one thing I do, forgetting those things which are behind and reaching forward to those things which are ahead, I press on toward the goal unto the prize of the high calling of God in Christ Jesus. (Philippians 3:13-14a)

I Can Always Triumph in Christ

Thanks be to God who always leads us in triumph in Christ Jesus, and through us diffuses the fragrance of his knowledge in every place. (2 Corinthians 2:14)

My Inheritance is in Jesus

When we receive Jesus as our Savior, we are born into the family of God. Jesus already died, so our inheritance is waiting to be received *now*, not after we die.

According to Ephesians 2:6, we are raised up together and made to sit in heavenly places in Christ Jesus. When we are in Christ, we become members of the family of God, and with that comes position, privileges, and a life of abundance in the spiritual realm. God's heavenly resources have been made available to us as believers here on Earth.

Our part is to accept this truth and receive it by faith. God doesn't force his benefits on anyone, and he won't withhold his blessings from those who take him at his Word. These scriptures reveal some of our inheritance.

May you be filled with joy, always thanking the Father, who has enabled you to share in the inheritance that belongs to his people who live in the light. (Colossians 1:12 NLT)

The Spirit himself bears witness with our spirit that we are children of God, and if children, then heirs of God and joint heirs with Christ. (Romans 8:16-17)

It is the living God, who gives us richly all things to enjoy. (I Timothy 6:17)

He who overcomes shall inherit all things, and I will be his God and he shall be my son. (Revelation 21:7)

"My sheep hear My voice, and I know them, and they follow Me." – John 10:27

CHAPTER NINE
Why am I Here?

People live their whole lives without knowing why they exist. Many have no idea God created them with a profound purpose. So, why am I here?

Everyone wants to be happy, but what makes us happy? Do possessions accomplish that goal? Not really. After we acquire so many things, they only become a burden. Does experiencing pleasure make us happy? Sure it does, for the moment. But pleasure doesn't last. We say, "Maybe if I become famous or powerful, I'll achieve the happiness I desire."

True happiness comes from understanding the real purpose for our being in the world at this time.

Our Purpose

> *Even before he made the world, God loved us and chose us in Christ to be holy and without fault in his eyes.*

> *God decided in advance to adopt us into his own family by bringing us to himself through Jesus Christ. This is what he wanted to do, and it gave him great pleasure.* (Ephesians 1:4-5 NLT)

I am Here to Have Fellowship with God

It's true. God wants to fellowship with us. Isn't that amazing? He wants us to talk to him and to know his voice when he speaks to us.

> *My sheep hear My voice, and I know them, and they follow Me.* (John 10:27)

> *Your ears shall hear a word behind you, saying, "This is the way, walk in it," whenever you turn to the right hand or whenever you turn to the left.* (Isaiah 30:21)

We have the privilege of knowing God's voice. He speaks in many ways. Usually, we hear him on the inside, like in our mind or heart. He will give us wisdom when we need direction. Sometimes he lavishes us with words of love, or a scripture might come to mind that's just right for our need. This is why it's so important to memorize Bible verses. We put God's Word inside so we can recognize we are hearing him when the verse we memorized lines up with what we heard as God's voice. God is always speaking, we just need to learn to listen.

> *I have hidden your word in my heart that I might not sin against you.* (Psalm 119:11)

Our relationship grows as we honor him with praise and worship.

> *You are holy, you inhabit the praises of your people.* (Psalm 22:3)

Isn't this verse great? God said when we praise him he is with us. Really, he is always with us, but there is something about praise and worship that makes his presence more real to us.

Sometimes, we hear God's voice through others, often without them even knowing they're answering our question, or confirming what we were seeking to know. He might speak through a billboard's words, or a song. The challenge is to learn to listen. The Holy Spirit is very creative and he enjoys surprising his children in the way he works.

I am Here to Live in God's Righteousness

> *For God took the sinless Christ and poured into him our sins. Then, in exchange, he poured God's goodness into us.* (2 Corinthians 5:21 TLB)

> *I, therefore, the prisoner of the Lord, beseech you to walk worthy of the calling with which you were called.* (Ephesians 4:1)

> *Whether you eat or drink, or whatever you do, do all to the glory of God.* (I Corinthians 10:31)

I am Here to Live Out God's Truth

> Jesus said, . . . *"Spend your energy seeking eternal life that the Son of Man can give you. For God the Father has given me the seal of approval."* They replied, *"We want to perform God's work, too. What should we do?"* Jesus told them, *"This is the only work God wants from you: Believe in the one he has sent."* (John 6:27-29 NLT)

I am Here to Make Disciples

> Jesus told his disciples *"I have been given all authority in heaven and on earth. Therefore, go and*

*make disciples of all the nations, baptizing them in
the name of the Father and the Son and the Holy
Spirit. Teach these new disciples to obey all the
commands I have given you. And be sure of this:
I am with you always, even to the end of the age.*
(Matthew 28:19-20 NLT)

I am Here to Demonstrate God's Power Working Through Me.

*Heal the sick, raise the dead, . . . drive out demons.
Freely you have received, freely give.* (Matthew 10:8)

I am Here to Share God's Love

*Jesus said, A new commandment I give to you, that
you love one another; as I have loved you, that you
also love one another. By this all will know that
you are my disciples, if you have love for one another.*
(John 13:34-35)

CHAPTER TEN

Love

○ ○ ○ ○ ○ ○ ○ ○

Love is the foundation of the Christian life because God IS Love. Therefore, when he comes to live in us, he gives us the ability to love with a lay-down-your-life-for-others kind of love.

> *He who does not love does not know God, for God is love.* (I John 4:8)

> *God so loved the world that he gave his only son, that whoever believes in him should not perish but have everlasting life.* (John 3:16)

> *If God so loved us, we also ought to love one another.* (I John 4:11)

> The first of all the commandments is: . . . *you shall love the Lord your God with all your heart, with all your soul, with all your mind, and with all your strength. This is the first commandment.*

And the second, like it, is this: You shall love your neighbor as yourself. There is no other commandment greater than these. (Mark 12:29-31)

There is no fear in love, but perfect love casts out fear, because fear involves torment. (I John 4:18)

I Corinthians 13:1-10, 13:

If I could speak all the languages of earth and of angels, but didn't love others, I would only be a noisy gong or a clanging cymbal.

If I understood all of God's secret plans and possessed all knowledge, and if I had such faith that I could move mountains, but didn't love others, I would be nothing.

If I gave everything I have to the poor and even sacrificed my body, I could boast about it, but if I didn't love others, I would have gained nothing.

Love is patient and kind. Love is not jealous or boastful or proud or rude. It does not demand its own way. It is not irritable, and it keeps no record of being wronged. It does not rejoice about injustice but rejoices whenever the truth wins out. Love never gives up, never loses faith, is always hopeful, and endures through every circumstance.

Prophecy and speaking in unknown languages and special knowledge will become useless. But love will last forever! Now our knowledge is partial and incomplete, and even the gift of prophecy reveals only part of the whole picture! But when the time of perfection comes, these partial things will become useless.

Three things will last forever, faith, hope, and love, and the greatest of these is love. (New Living Translation)

CHAPTER ELEVEN
Tell Me About Prayer

○ ○ ○ ○ ○ ○ ○ ○ ○

God blessed us with the privilege of coming to him with our needs. But prayer is much more than asking him to do things. As we learn to pray we come to know him better. The life of prayer is an intimate adventure into the heart of God.

When Jesus' disciples came to him asking how they should pray, he gave them what we call The Lord's Prayer as his perfect example. Let's look at each sentence to see what we can learn.

THE LORD'S PRAYER

Our Father in heaven, hallowed (or holy) is your name.
The very first line reminds us that when we pray, we need to stop and remind ourselves who God is. He is our holy Father, creator of all things.

As we think about how awesome it is to have the privilege of praying to him, we're inspired to thank and worship him for who he is. Isn't that perfect?

Your kingdom come, your will be done on earth as it is in heaven.
Jesus told us to ask our heavenly Father to make earth like heaven. Have you examined what heaven is like yet? I get excited thinking about the fact that it's God's will for me to pray heaven to earth. How about you?

Give us this day our daily bread.
God is so good. He wants to provide for all our needs. We work so hard to get all the things we think we want and need. God's Word says he gives abundantly above anything we could hope or ask. Of course, that promise, found in Ephesians 3:20, comes with a stipulation - according to the Holy Spirit's power that works in us.

. . . and forgive us our debts, as we forgive our debtors.
Oh my; there's another stipulation. If we want our Father to forgive us, we need to do some forgiving. Who does this thought bring to mind?

And do not lead us into temptation but deliver us from the evil one.
Our God is all powerful. He can deliver us from anything holding us captive. When we're desperate enough to seek him for freedom, he is faithful to answer. The evil one only has power over us in the areas we, or our bloodline, have allowed.

For yours is the kingdom and the power and the glory forever.
After all is said and done, and we've finished chasing rainbows, we will look up and know God and his kingdom, power, and glory are the final word for all that we really want.

Amen.
Amen means let these things be so. No better word is needed.

Yet, the subject of prayer is huge. But, instead of telling of lofty ideals found in a prayer life, let's remember, God says we are his children, and he is a good Father who wants a relationship with us. He listens when we pray.

Praying can be very simple. God answered Paul's prayer when all he said was, *"Lord, save me!"* (Matthew 14:30 NLT)

God looks at the heart. A desperate prayer of faith has much more power than hours of many words. Profound prayers can be as simple as, "God!" He sees our heart and knows everything about the situation we want him involved in.

Now, after sharing those words, here are some verses to show a maturing that comes as we learn to pray.

> *Pray in the Spirit at all times and on every occasion. Stay alert and be persistent in your prayers for all believers everywhere.* (Ephesians 6:18 NIV)
>
> *Keep watch and pray, so that you will not give in to temptation. For the spirit is willing, but the body is weak.* (Matthew 26:41 NLT)

Here are a few tools for our prayer belt.

Worship

When we worship God, heaven and earth unite and we enter into the possibilities of God's kingdom world.

The Word

The Word is a powerful tool in prayer. As we memorize scriptures, they're hidden in our hearts so the Holy Spirit can bring them to our minds to help us know how to pray.

Jesus' blood

It's sad that the power of the blood of Jesus isn't taught much anymore because his blood sacrifice still gives us powerful protection, and restores lives and situations.

Without the shedding of blood there is no forgiveness. (Hebrews 9:22)

If we walk in the light as he is in the light, we have fellowship with one another and the blood of Jesus Christ his son cleanses us from all sin. (I John 1:7)

They overcame by the blood of the Lamb and by the word of their testimony, (Revelation 12:11)

You were not redeemed with corruptible things, like silver or gold, from your aimless conduct received by tradition from your father. But with the precious blood of Jesus, as of a lamb without blemish and without spots. (I Peter 1:18-19)

Since we have been made right in God's sight by the blood of Jesus, he will certainly save us from God's condemnation. For since our friendship with God was restored by the death of his Son while we were still his enemies, we will certainly be saved through the life of his son. (Romans 5:9 NLT)

Jesus' name

Therefore, God has highly exalted him and given him the name which is above every name, that at the name of Jesus every knee would bow of those in heaven and those on earth, and those under the earth. (Philippians 2:9)

Jesus' name is all powerful. That's why we use the words, "In Jesus' name," when we pray. His name is like putting a protective shield around our prayers.

His name makes hell quiver. We can remind the enemy that Jesus said all authority has been given to him in heaven and on earth. (Matthew 28:18)

Fasting and prayer

The Bible says some things only come out through fasting and prayer. Fasting is usually giving up food. There's nothing like giving up food to awaken our spirit. We can also fast bad habits or other pleasures – whatever the Holy Spirit directs us to do.

In Matthew 17:21 the disciples asked Jesus why they couldn't cast out the demons tormenting a boy. He said, This kind does not go out except by prayer and fasting.

> Psalm 35:13 says, . . . *when they were sick, . . .*
> *I humbled myself with fasting . . .*

"I will bless the Lord at all times. His praise will continually be in my mouth." – Psalm 34:1

CHAPTER TWELVE
Baptism

ᵒ ᵒ ᵒ ᵒ ᵒ ᵒ ᵒ ᵒ ᵒ

Why should I be baptized?

Baptism announces to everyone, including heaven and hell that we have received a new life as a Christian, and we now live under the covering of the Kingdom of God. Baptism doesn't make us a believer. It confirms we already believe. Baptism doesn't save us; only our faith in Christ does that. Baptism is more like a wedding ring. We follow Jesus' example with an outward symbol of the commitment we've made in our heart.

> *By baptism, we were buried with him and share his death, in order that, just as Christ was raised from the dead. . . so also we may live a new life.* (Romans 6:4)

When someone becomes a Christian he becomes a brand new person inside.

> *The old life has passed away and a new life has begun.* (2 Corinthians 5:17)

You were buried with Christ when you were baptized. And with him you were raised to new life because you trusted the mighty power of God, who raised Jesus from the dead. (Colossians 2:12 NLT)

After we repent of sins and receive Jesus as Savior, the Bible says we are to be baptized. We follow Jesus' example.

At that time Jesus came from Nazareth and was baptized by John in the river. (Mark 1:9)

CHAPTER THIRTEEN

Communion

⚬ ⚬ ⚬ ⚬ ⚬ ⚬ ⚬

Just as the first church, we the people of God practice communion to honor Jesus and remind ourselves of the price he paid for our salvation. The bread represents the suffering he endured for our healing. (Isaiah 53:5) The wine reminds us of his spilt blood, which was God's requirement as the perfect sacrifice for our sins, so we could be righteous before him.

Here's a verse to describe communion:

> On the night when he was betrayed, the Lord Jesus took some bread and gave thanks to God for it. Then he broke it in pieces and said, "This is my body, which is for you. Do this in remembrance of me." In the same way, he took the cup of wine after supper, saying, "This cup is the new covenant between God and his people. An agreement confirmed with my blood. Do this to remember me as often as you drink it. For every

time you eat this bread and drink this cup, you are announcing the Lord's death until he comes again. (I Corinthians 11:23-26 NLT)

We are made whole through Jesus' sacrifice.

He bore our sins in his own body on the tree, that we, having died to sins, might live for righteousness–by whose stripes you were healed. (I Peter 2:24)

He was pierced for our rebellion, crushed for our sins. He was beaten so we could be whole. He was whipped so we could be healed. (Isaiah 53:5 NLT)

Communion is only for those who receive Jesus as Savior.

Anyone who eats and drinks without recognizing the body of the Lord eats and drinks judgment on himself. (I Corinthians 11:29)

CHAPTER FOURTEEN
Why Worship?

○ ○ ○ ○ ○ ○ ○

Because of who God is, we worship him. We recognize and honor him with words of praise, and with songs and music. And it's interesting that when we turn our eyes on our Father, our troubles become much smaller.

> *I called upon the Lord, who is worthy of praise, and he saved me from my enemies.* (Psalm 18:3 NLT)

> *Then I looked, and I heard the voice of many angels around the throne, the living creatures, and the elders; and the number of them was ten thousand times ten thousand, and thousands of thousands, saying with a loud voice, 'Worthy is the Lamb who was slain to receive power, and riches, and wisdom, and strength, and honor, and glory, and blessing.'* (Revelation 5:11-12)

We need to change the way we see God. This verse reminds us that God is mighty, glorious, and present. As we worship him we become more aware of this fact.

Praise and Worship reminds us who we are.

> *You, as living stones, are being built up as a spiritual house, a holy priesthood, to offer up spiritual sacrifices acceptable to God through Jesus Christ as a chosen generation, a royal priesthood, a holy nation. His own special people, that you may proclaim the praises of him who called you out of darkness into his marvelous light. (I Peter 2:5, 9 NLT)*

All of nature praises God. We are remiss if we don't worship him.

> *Let everything that has breath praise the Lord. (Psalm 150:6)*

Praise and worship helps free us

> *Put on a garment of praise for the spirit of heaviness. (Isaiah 61:3)*

> *From the lips of children and infants you have ordained praise because of your enemies, to silence the foe and the avenger. (Psalm 8:2)*

> *. . . Be filled with the Holy Spirit, singing psalms and hymns and spiritual songs among yourselves, and making music to the Lord in your heart. And give thanks for everything to God the Father in the name of our Lord Jesus Christ. (Ephesians 5:19-20)*

And let's not forget. When we praise and worship, God's presence is always with us.

> *My God, you are holy, enthroned in the praises of your people. (Psalm 22:3)*

CHAPTER FIFTEEN
Heaven and Hell

Perhaps by now you're saying, "Okay, but, what's the deal about heaven and hell?" Let's look at a few verses to see what God's divine Word reveals on those subjects.

Heaven is God's kingdom. Scriptures give us a glimpse of what it's like. Heaven is full of wonders beyond anything we can understand, but even better, God is there in all of his majesty.

When we ask Jesus to come into our life, we know our name is written in heaven's Book of Life.

> . . .Rejoice because your names are written in Heaven. (Luke 10:20)

> All who are victorious will be clothed in white. I will never erase their names from the Book of Life, but I

will announce before my Father and his angels that they are mine. (Revelation 3:6 NLT)

I tell you the truth, everyone who acknowledges me publicly here on earth, the Son of Man will also acknowledge in the presence of God's angels. (Luke 12:8 NLT)

God will wipe every tear from their eyes, and there will be no more death or sorrow or crying or pain. All these things are gone forever. And the one sitting on the throne said, "Look, I am making everything new!" And then he said to me, "Write this down, for what I tell you is trustworthy and true. And he also said, "It is finished! I am the Alpha and the Omega, the Beginning and the End. To all who are thirsty I will give freely from the springs of the water of life. All who are victorious will inherit all these blessings, and I will be their God, and they will be my children. (Revelation 21:4-7)

HELL

To think of Hell is to think of the exact opposite of Heaven. No love or any virtue of God dwells there.

But the cowardly, unbelieving, abominable, murderers, sexually immoral, sorcerers, idolaters, and all liars shall have their part in the lake that burns with fire and brimstone, which is the second death. (Revelation 21:8)

A person is a fool to store up earthly wealth but not have a rich relationship with God. (Luke 12:21 NKJV)

There really is a place called Hell. The concept can run from a pit somewhere below where fire and brimstones burn, and the people cry out in torment, to what some describe as "the absence of God's presence." That would be Hell as well. We do know it's where Satan rules. That's bad enough for me not to want to go there.

> *So it will be at the end of the age. The angels will come forth, separate the wicked from among the just and cast them into the furnace of fire. There will be wailing and gnashing of teeth.* (Matthew 13:49-50)

> *These shall be punished with everlasting destruction from the presence of the Lord and from the glory of his power.* (2 Thessalonians 1:9)

> *Depart from me, you who are cursed, into the eternal fire prepared for the devil and his angels.* (Matthew 25:41)

> *God did not spare angels when they sinned, but sent them to hell, putting them in chains of darkness to be held for judgment. . .* (2 Peter 2:4)

> *Blessed is the man who delights in the Lord and his commandments. . . The wicked will see it (the blessings of the righteous) and be grieved; he will gnash his teeth and melt away; the desire of the wicked shall perish.* (Psalm 112:10)

Psalm 112 tells of the blessings of righteousness, so you might want to read the whole chapter.

God is always victorious

> *Death is swallowed up in victory. O Death, where is your victory? O Death, where is your sting?* (I Corinthians 15:54b-55 NLT)

> *For the law of the Spirit of life in Christ Jesus has made me free from the law of sin and death.* (Romans 8:2)

"Your ears shall hear a word behind you, saying, "This is the way, walk in it;" whenever you turn to the right hand or whenever you turn to the left."
– Isaiah 30:21

CHAPTER SIXTEEN

Not the End, But the Beginning

Now we have a little understanding of what it means to believe in Jesus as our Savior, and be called a Christian (Christ-in-me). But this is only the beginning of learning to live in the fullness of the amazing life our Creator, who loves us without measure, offers.

Enjoy the journey. Let your faith grow as you trust God in every trial and victory you face. Live life fully knowing the Holy Spirit is always with you. Dream big. God has plans for your life that are bigger and better than anything you can imagine.

> *The Lord bless you and keep you; the Lord make his face shine upon you. And be gracious to you. The Lord lift up his countenance upon you and give you peace.* (Numbers 6:24-26)

"The Lord bless you and keep you; the Lord make his face shine upon you. And be gracious to you. The Lord lift up his countenance upon you and give you peace." – Numbers 6:24-26

Made in the USA
Columbia, SC
03 April 2021